# BASERUNNING

# THE WINNING EDGE
# BASERUNNING

By BOB CLUCK

Foreword by STEVE SAX

CONTEMPORARY
BOOKS, INC.
CHICAGO • NEW YORK

**Library of Congress Cataloging-in-Publication Data**

Cluck, Bob.
The winning edge : baserunning.

1. Base running (Baseball)—Juvenile literature.
I. Title.
GV868.C55 1987 796.357'27 86-32941
ISBN 0-8092-4784-4 (pbk.)

All photos courtesy Teri Cluck Photography
Equipment courtesy San Diego School of Baseball


Published by Contemporary Books, Inc.
180 North Michigan Avenue, Chicago, Illinois 60601
Manufactured in the United States of America
Library of Congress Catalog Card Number: 86-32941
International Standard Book Number: 0-8092-4784-4

Published simultaneously in Canada by Beaverbooks, Ltd.
195 Allstate Parkway, Valleywood Business Park
Markham, Ontario L3R 4T8 Canada

*To Teri, Jennifer, and Amber*
*for patience during the long road trips*
*and the film sessions at home*
*over 20 great years*

# Contents

# Foreword

Baseball tradition has always glorified its great sluggers—guys like Babe Ruth, Hank Aaron, and Reggie Jackson—for good reason. There's nothing more exciting than watching that little white ball disappear into the faraway bleachers.

But at 5′11″ and 185 pounds, home runs will never make me famous. Instead, my game is predicated on hustle and aggressiveness to do the important "little" things that help the Dodgers win. One of the most important—and often overlooked—baseball skills is baserunning. In a close game where every run counts, good baserunning will often be the deciding factor. Getting to first isn't always enough: mental lapses on the base paths can be as costly as they are embarrassing.

When I arrived in the big leagues to stay in 1981, people likened me to Pete Rose because of the way I ran out bases on balls. Well, I admire Pete, but I never patterned my game after him or anyone else. If it looks like I play baseball as if I'm having the time of my life, it's because I am. I'm glad to know that hustle (and often its end result—a dirty uniform) has become a trademark of mine.

It's wrong for kids to think that you have to be fast to be a good base runner. While speed certainly provides an advantage, astute concentration, keen awareness, and fine attention to fundamentals is equally important. Remember in 1974 when Charles O. Finley, owner of the Oakland A's, signed a world-class sprinter named Herb Washington to be his club's designated runner? Even the fastest guy in the world had trouble excelling as a specialist in a foreign sport. In fact, lack of experience probably resulted in his being picked off in key situations—including once in the World Series. Nothing kills a rally or takes away offensive momentum faster than baserunning mishaps.

Guys like Maury Wills, Lou Brock, and Rickey Henderson receive tremendous publicity because of their stolen-base records. Indeed, they are all great base runners. But baserunning, as the pros know it, is much more than stealing second. Consummate base runners, the guys with the capability to affect the outcome of ballgames, will take the extra base, on a hit or an out, when the situation allows for it. Hustle and determination like this can subtly change the pulse of the game, rattle the pitcher, and mess up his timing.

I set the Dodgers' rookie record for steals in a season with 49 in 1982. In just five full major league seasons I rank sixth on the club's all-time stolen-base list. I'm proud too that only once have I scored less than 70 runs in a season. My job is to get on base and make something happen. When I do—and when I score—the Dodgers have a better chance of winning.

Baseball is unique because you don't have to be in possession of the ball to score a point for your team. That's why baserunning shouldn't be taken for granted.

The next time you watch your favorite slugger smash a long homerun, see if anyone scores ahead of him. That's the easiest way to run the bases.

*Steve Sax*
*Los Angeles Dodgers*

# 1
# The Successful Baserunner

Baserunning has always been an underrated part of baseball. More games are won and lost on baserunning than most people might think. The small things that win ball games go unnoticed by the baseball novice. We will break down and analyze the offensive game so that you can use some of the techniques found here to improve this important part of the game.

Everyone in major league baseball talks about speed and its value to a ballclub. But some of the finest base runners in history could not run fast. And some of the fastest men in baseball are not skilled base runners and often make foolish mistakes. Anyone on a team can and should become a good base runner. It requires intelligence, observation, and concentration.

One popular theory is that baserunning is strictly instinctive and can't be taught successfully. However, most good baseball people realize that baserunning skills can be greatly improved with hard work. It's funny that ballplayers known to have good "instincts" are also the players who are the most intelligent and who spend the most time working on their skills.

The one area of the game in which fans rate a player's effort is on the bases. When a player runs out every ball to first, takes an extra base, and is generally aggressive, he quickly becomes a favorite with the fans. When a player is lazy, the first area that it shows up in is his baserunning.

Becoming a good base runner is hard work, and no player should take the task lightly. Players who think it is not an important part of the game never become good players. The techniques we describe are tried and true, and will give the base runner from Little League to professional ball an edge when game time comes.

A good base runner always knows the game situation and what his run might represent to the team. How a runner reacts to any situation depends on many factors. Certainly the number of outs is important. The score, where other runners are on the bases, where the defense is playing, and the pitcher's tendencies are all involved. To take advantage of all these factors and to display good judgment, you can't suddenly start paying attention when you arrive at first base.

When you are on the bench, or between innings of a game in which you aren't playing, you must watch the defense constantly. It is amazing what you can pick up from the other club when you pay close attention. You and your teammates can use this information to take advantage of the other team when the situation develops. The information you gain can be passed around the team so everyone can benefit.

Most players are not aggressive enough because they either don't know what to do or they're afraid to fail, or both. A good baseball coach will never be critical of a player who tries to take an extra base and is thrown out trying to be aggressive. Of course, good judgment should always be used, and again, the player who takes baserunning seriously usually has the best judgment.

Rules such as not making the first or third out at third base, or not advancing to third from second when a ball is hit to the third-base side with less than two outs are just general rules. These rules should not be taken lightly but should never take away a player's aggressiveness in these situations.

# QUALITIES THAT GOOD BASE RUNNERS HAVE IN COMMON

- Good base runners are aggressive within the confines of good judgment.
- They always know the game situation and what their particular run represents.
- Good base runners realize that the little things on the bases are the things that win ball games.
- They are constantly watching the other team to pick up tendencies they can use to their advantage.
- Good base runners know that speed helps, but that it is not a requirement for good skills on the bases.
- They know their limitations, and by thinking of the team first avoid foolish mistakes.
- Good base runners are never satisfied with one base and always think one base ahead.

# 2
# Running Around the Bases

At the instant your bat hits the ball, you become what is called the "batter-runner." The speed at which you can round the bases is a product of proper running and baserunning techniques, God-given ability, and effort.

## RUNNING TECHNIQUES

All of us are blessed with a certain amount of foot-speed, and most experts agree that this speed can be improved within limitations. Certain fundamentals are often violated by most young runners, and if corrected can make a substantial difference.

Many runners swing their arms improperly, and the result is an overall loss of body coordination and, of course, speed. Your arms should not rotate across your body, but instead pump alongside your body. Your left arm should extend when your right leg extends, and vice versa. Your body should lean forward when you're sprinting, and your hands and face should be relaxed. These fundamentals are taught by track coaches across the nation.

*When you run properly, your arms should not swing from side to side across your body.*

*Your left arm should extend forward when your right foot is forward, and your right arm should extend when your left foot is forward.*

*Your body should lean forward when you sprint.*

# RUNNING THROUGH THE BAG

When you run to first after hitting the ball, the primary concern is hustle. Many players simply don't hustle down the line to first when it appears they've hit an easy out. It is not too much to ask that a player run hard to first base every time. Believe me, the fans will notice a player who doesn't hustle on the bases.

You should go past first base by at least 15 to 20 feet. If you're able to stop before that, you probably slow down before you cross the base. There is also a chance for injury if you try to stop too soon. When you approach the bag, zero in on the bag and make sure you touch it in the middle or on the front edge. Don't jump at the bag on a close play. It not only slows you down but there is a good chance for injury.

When the ball is overthrown, if you make any break toward second base, you can be tagged out. A smart player uses his coach, but more important you should know the field (how far the fence is and what kind it is) and the game situation.

*Run hard and touch the bag in the middle or on the front edge.*

*Jumping not only slows you down but increases the risk of injury.*

*Run past first base and slow down naturally.*

*Any break toward second can result in your being tagged out; make sure you can make it to second before making a break of any kind.*

# MAKING TURNS

At all the bases, there is a right and wrong way to make turns. Baserunning, unlike all other skills in baseball, is a fairly exact science. Since we are dealing with angles and measurable distances, there are some conclusions we can draw from close observations.

Execute a turn by heading for one spot and making one "cut." The spot will vary from runner to runner and base to base. For instance, at first base, the spot is usually about five feet to the right of the bag. From the time you know the ball is through the infield and a turn is in order, you should head directly for the spot. Most of the time you will see the ball go through the infield or you will know you've hit the ball to the outfield. Some people will tell you not to look at the ball at all, but let's not kid each other; everybody looks at the ball during their first few steps. It is not wise, however, to look at the ball too long.

Upon reaching the spot, lean to the left to help cut down the angle. Touch the bag with whichever foot comes up in stride rather than break stride to touch it with one foot or the other. Make a good aggressive turn, especially on the base hit to center or left field. If the hit is to right field, keep your turn to a minimum for obvious reasons (you may get thrown out). An aggressive turn around first will allow you to take the extra base if the ball is mishandled. Runners who make wide turns will also force the defense into mistakes because they will hurry their plays. If you're thinking "two" from the time you leave the batter's box, an aggressive turn will result. Your job is to make the outfielder stop you by making the play cleanly and throwing accurately to the relay man. If there is hesitation or a slight mistake, you won't even have to break stride if you've made an aggressive turn. Many players are thrown out trying to stretch a single into a double, not because it was a bad idea but because they didn't make a good turn before the defensive mistake occurred.

*Head for a spot about five feet to the right of first base.*

*When you are about 15 feet from the spot, start to lean left to help cut down the angle of the turn.*

*Touch the bag on the inside corner with whichever foot comes up in stride.*

*When the ball is in left field or center field, your turn should be extremely aggressive and may even force the defense into mistakes; you should think, "Let's see if you can stop me."*

*Your turn should be somewhat shorter when the base hit is to right field, in case the outfielder throws behind you (remember, the rightfielder usually has the strongest arm in the outfield).*

*Always think one base ahead, and with an aggressive turn you'll never have to break stride to go for second in case of a defensive lapse.*

*When you return to first after making the turn, watch the relay back into the infield instead of retreating to first blindly.*

# 3
# Breaks and Leads

## THE PRIMARY LEADS

When you arrive at first, your first thoughts should be about what your run might represent and other game situations. Look at the coach for a sign and check the defense to see where the outfielders and infielders are playing. Think about the pitcher's pickoff move and the catcher's throwing ability. Only after you've considered all of this do you begin to assume your lead.

# 10 QUESTIONS YOU SHOULD ASK YOURSELF BEFORE YOU BEGIN TO TAKE A LEAD

1. How many outs?
2. Are there other runners on base?
3. What is the score, and what does my run represent?
4. Is the coach giving me a sign?
5. Where are the outfielders and infielders playing?
6. What is the pitcher's pickoff move like?
7. Does the catcher like to try pickoffs, and does he have a strong arm?
8. Does this team have any special defensive plays I should be aware of?
9. Where is my teammate (the next hitter) likely to hit the ball?
10. What kind of lead will I take with all these other factors in mind?

## Breaks and Leads

While watching the pitcher and only the pitcher, you begin to assume your lead. With a definite spot (distance from the bag) in mind, you step first with your right foot, then bring your left foot up to meet the right (keeping your feet shoulder width apart at all times). Continue until you reach the distance from the bag that you planned. There is no reason for you to look back at the bag if you're counting your steps (this requires some practice time). Remain slightly crouched while taking your lead and never jump or cross your feet.

The average lead is nine or ten feet off the bag, and when you can get more than that you're doing a great job. Most runners have a fear of getting picked off and coaches have a tough time getting them to take a good lead. Getting a good aggressive lead is a product of practice and having the confidence that you can get back. Of course, your lead will vary somewhat from pitcher to pitcher and with the game situation. By practicing the steps, you will be able to assume your nine-foot lead, your eleven-foot lead, and your twelve-foot lead easily.

*Extend your right foot first, with the left following and closing the distance (never getting closer than shoulder width).*

*Never look back at the bag while taking a lead.*

*Never jump when taking a lead; remain slightly crouched and under control.*

*Crossing your feet will leave you in an unbalanced position and should be avoided at all costs.*

If the pitcher does make a move to first, you will go back in one of two ways. If you have a substantial lead, you will probably go in head first. Touch the bag with your right hand on the rear corner. Keep your face to the outfield side so the ball (or the tag) won't hit you in the face.

If you go into the bag standing up, you have two options. First, you can go in with your right foot on the bag, which requires three steps. The first step is a crossover with your right foot. Then you take a step with your left, then a step with your right to the bag.

Or you can cross over with your right and step on the bag with your left foot, simply bringing around the right foot for balance.

*If your lead is substantial, go back headfirst, with your right hand on the bag and your face to the outfield side.*

*One way to go back standing up is with your right foot (three steps to the bag).*

# SECONDARY LEADS

When the pitch is made to the plate, you must gain some ground and assume your "secondary lead." Some players are satisfied with taking a little step or two and watching the ball approach the plate. The good base runner takes an aggressive secondary lead by using a crossover step, a hop, and then coming down with his weight on the right foot as the ball crosses the plate (remember that the ball is in flight to the plate while this maneuver is taking place).

If your timing is right and if the ball is either hit or gets away from the catcher, you will be able to cross over and break to the next base without losing momentum. This timing takes lots of practice and will only be developed if you spend time on the bases practicing it. After you come down on your right leg and the ball is not hit, you must take a couple of quick steps back toward the base to avoid being picked off (if you're assuming a good secondary lead, you will be in jeopardy of being picked off by the catcher after the pitch). After a couple of quick steps you can relax if there is no play on.

When the ball is hit in the air you will either go back and tag up or go to what is described as halfway position. If you go halfway and the ball is caught, retreat to the bag quickly and watch the throws that follow the catch. Many times there is an opportunity to advance on these throws, but you will miss it if you return to the base blindly.

Always be alert for pitches in the dirt or pitches that otherwise get away from the catcher. When the catcher goes to his knees to block a ball, the ball need not get away from him very far for the alert runner to advance.

## THE CROSSOVER STEP

The crossover step is a basic movement used in baseball to move to one side or the other. It is nothing more than a movement to save time in going laterally. First your right foot pivots slightly (opens up), and your left foot then comes across your body and takes a full stride in the desired direction. There is difference of opinion in many areas of baseball, but almost everyone uses the crossover step on the bases and in the field.

*To take a secondary lead, use a crossover step, a hop, and have your weight come down on your right foot as the ball crosses the plate. If the ball is hit, you can cross over toward the next base without losing momentum.*

343

# LEADS FROM SECOND BASE

Leads from second and third are each different from the lead from first. There are different factors to be considered with each lead. However, you should still go through your checklist of questions about game situations, etc.

The lead from second could be called a "safe maximum" lead in that it is both a safe lead and a lead from which you can score. Remember that second base is called "scoring position" for good reason. We must compromise some safety to get a good jump and score.

The length of your lead is determined by your quickness, the pitcher's move, the catcher's throwing ability, and the importance of your potential run.

This safe maximum lead is a distance from second that you cannot be picked off from. *The idea here is that we don't want to sacrifice the runner for a few more feet of lead.*

You can't let the infielders disturb you. If they force you back toward second, you will likely miss a scoring opportunity.

Using the safe maximum lead makes it unnecessary for the third-base coach to give voice commands when the middle infielders jockey in and out trying to disturb you. With a big crowd, the voice commands are useless anyway. You need only watch the pitcher and forget about what the shortstop and second baseman are doing. You will score or not score the run based on your jump. The jump should be measured from your secondary lead and not your primary lead. The player who has the ability to steal third should modify this system to fit him.

The general rule is that the ball should go through the infield if it is hit in front of you (to the third-base side of the field) before you take off with less than two outs. This should not be a hard-and-fast rule. You can advance from second base on lots of balls that are in front of you. Whenever the third baseman has to either retreat into the hole or come in for a high chopper there is ample opportunity to advance.

# WHEN LEADING OFF FROM SECOND BASE, YOU SHOULD

- Assume a comfortable "safe maximum" lead from which you can't be picked off by the pitcher or catcher (never take your eyes off the pitcher during this lead).
- Work hard at covering distance during your secondary lead.
- Make sure your right foot is coming down as the ball crosses home plate.
- Take two quick steps back if the catcher catches the ball cleanly.

Remember that you *should* be in jeopardy after you take your secondary lead if you've been aggressive enough. Don't worry about getting picked off by the catcher on a pitchout. The runner at second is the first one in the ballpark to know a pitchout is coming (from the early movement of the catcher).

*Assume a "safe maximum" lead that you can't be picked off from, but that can get you a great jump when you try to score.*

*You will score more easily if your secondary lead off second base is aggressive.*

# LEADS FROM THIRD BASE

The lead from third is a "walking lead." Begin with a lead approximately the same distance the third baseman is off the bag. Walk from there two or three steps as the pitch is on its way to the plate. Use the same secondary-lead principle and land on your right foot as the ball is crossing the plate. Take two quick steps back when the ball is not hit and the catcher handles it cleanly. When on third, take your lead in foul territory and return in fair territory. The catcher can't tell how far you're off the bag when you take this route.

The game situation and the positioning of the infielders will dictate how aggressive you can be. If the infield is in, let the ball go through the infield before you break for the plate. If the infield is back or halfway, the coach or manager may elect to have you "go on contact." This simply means that you break for the plate on any ball that is hit. The offense is taking a chance that even if the ball is hit to an infielder, your great jump off third will allow you to beat the play at home. This play is widely used in the major leagues and throughout baseball's higher levels.

On the "squeeze play," wait for the pitcher's arm to start forward (when his stride foot hits the ground) before you break for the plate.

*Use what is called a "walking lead" from third base, with your weight coming down on your right foot when the ball crosses the plate.*

*On the squeeze play don't break from third until the pitcher's arm has started forward or until his stride foot is planted (he can't change direction at this point).*

# TAGGING UP

Runners on all the bases should tag up and advance as much as possible. Whenever a fly ball is in foul territory all runners should be tagging up. When you tag up at any base, never leave early; you're sure to get caught.

Tagging up at first on a long fly ball with no outs is an advanced play for most youth-league players. Tagging up at second with no outs or one out is a good play and should be encouraged on any team.

When tagging up, watch the fielder closely and evaluate your chances of advancing based on four factors:

1. **What does your run represent?**
2. **How deep is the ball hit?**
3. **How strong is the fielder's throwing arm?**
4. **What kind of position is he in when he catches it?**

Often, as the fielder catches the ball, he moves into a poor position (back on his heels, etc.) that might allow you to advance on a ball that is normally not deep enough. You must also be alert on the relay that may follow a fly ball. If the relay is mishandled, you have an excellent opportunity to advance.

*When tagging up assume a position that allows you to break as soon as the ball is caught.*

# 4

# Base Stealing and Hit-and-Run Plays

## WORKING FOR A LEAD

If you're a potential base stealer, you must go for more than the average runner in terms of primary lead. You can't be satisfied with the nine or ten feet from first base that the average runner is satisfied with. You must work at getting two, three, or four extra feet in order to be able to steal. Consider it a battle between you and the pitcher. Chances are that the advantage you might gain on your lead will be a major factor in whether you're out or safe at second or third.

# THE PITCHER'S MOVES

Most pitchers, especially at the lower levels, have deliveries that are easy to steal on. There are certain characteristics that indicate when a pitcher is going to try a pickoff move or throw to home plate.

Right-handed pitchers rely on quickness as their major weapon against the potential base stealer. The ones who aren't quick must wear the runner down by driving him back time after time with throws to first. Watch the front (left) shoulder of the right-handed pitcher for an indication of when he might go to the plate or to first. When the shoulder closes (moves away from you), he is going to the plate, and when it opens toward you, the pitcher is coming to first. If the pitcher begins to close his front shoulder and then throws to first it is a balk. The base stealer must know the pitchers he faces and which ones are apt to try this illegal move. A balk should also be called when the pitcher fails to step toward first base with his left foot when making a throw. In addition, the pitcher can't fake a throw to first while on the rubber, or otherwise deceive the runner.

*The right-hander closes his front shoulder to go to the plate.*

*When the right-handed pitcher opens his left shoulder toward the runner he is throwing to first base.*

*The pitcher must step toward first base with his left foot on a pickoff attempt.*

Left-handers will either have great moves or will be easy to steal on. The left-hander who gives things away will usually do it in one of two ways. He will raise his leg and look to home and throw to first, or look to first and throw home. As a base stealer you can get back when he starts the leg kick and is looking toward the plate. The other area in which left-handers give their move away is in the point when going to first and a different point when going home. This is a bit tougher to read than the head movement.

Since most left-handers are so tough, lots of base stealers are now taking shorter leads (to make the pitcher think they're not stealing), and going on the pitcher's first movement (when he starts to bring up the leg).

---

*Some left-handers look home and throw to first or look to first and throw home.*

*Most left-handers will kick and "close off" when going to the plate.*

*Some left-handers give away their move to first when they kick their leg and don't "close off."*

# STEALING SITUATIONS

The situation will always dictate whether or not a steal is in order. When you are on your own to steal at will, the monkey is on your back. Most of the time, you will get your signs from the coach or manager. It is not wise to steal when your team is behind too far or ahead too far. It is simply not a good percentage play when you are behind more than four or five runs, and sometimes the other team becomes aroused when you steal with an eight- or nine-run lead. The only hard-and-fast rule is: *Can you help your team with a steal in this situation?*

When players reach the higher levels, they start trying to steal on a count that is likely to produce a curveball or other off-speed pitch. The top base stealers in the major leagues will usually go on one of the first two pitches and won't wait for any particular pitch or count. The best stealers are successful 80 percent of the time, or so. If you aren't successful more than half of the time, you're probably going too often to help the club.

# 5
# Efficient and Safe Sliding Techniques

## THE BENT-LEG SLIDE

Sliding is one of the fun things in baseball, but it can be dangerous. Many different sliding techniques are used. There are hook slides, pop-up slides, etc., that all look great but are not necessarily a good idea. The basic slide that most other slides have developed from is the straight-in, "bent-leg" slide.

When you learn baseball skills, you need to develop this slide early on. This is the slide used in the major leagues nearly 90 percent of the time. It is used to make routine slides into bases on force plays, it is used to break up double plays, and it should be used going into home plate and any other time a slide is appropriate. There are some important rules concerning sliding that every player and coach should know.

# IMPORTANT FACTS CONCERNING SLIDING

- On any close play, when in doubt, SLIDE!!!
- Never slow down or be tentative with a slide; go into the base at full speed.
- Slide early, never late.
- Go straight into the bag or to the area that you have committed to; many runners are hurt trying to avoid tags in the middle of a slide.
- Never put one hand down to brace yourself; keep your hands up during the slide.
- Your lead leg, not the one that is bent underneath, should touch the bag.
- Even when breaking up double plays, never go in with the intent to hurt someone; not only is it a display of poor sportsmanship but you may end up injuring yourself.

## Efficient and Safe Sliding Techniques

When you're learning to slide, practice on grass and without shoes. When you become more comfortable you can try it on the dirt with shoes. You can also spread out cardboard boxes and slide on them. It is both fun and effective to sprinkle the grass with water and slide on that just to get the feel of getting down. Once the initial fear is gone, sliding is nothing but fun.

The outside of your calf and the buttocks will absorb the shock when you slide. If you turn to the side and land on your hip, you probably get those round red welts on your side regularly. Because of their appearance, these are called "strawberries." They seem never to heal, and just about the time they develop a nice scab, here comes another slide and there they are again. Sliding pads will help, but the bottom line is: *If you learn to slide properly, you won't get strawberries.*

Injuries occur because of improper technique and for no other reason. The most common cause is putting your hand down, which in turn will rotate your body to the side just before you hit the ground. Your hip bone hits the ground, and the skin between the bone and the ground is scraped away (ouch). As long as you use the natural padding on your rear end, no injury should be sustained.

*When you put your hand down, your hip bone hits the ground, causing a "strawberry."*

*Hold your hands up during the slide.*

*In a properly executed slide, the outside of the calf hits the ground first, then the shock is absorbed by the buttocks.*

*Don't slide into the base and touch the bag with your bent leg.*

*Touch the bag with your lead leg when sliding into a base.*

# BREAKING UP DOUBLE PLAYS

Breaking up double plays is a part of the game that is necessary, but for the most part it's either ignored or overdone. Some players do it with the intent to hurt someone, while others go in as if it were just a simple force play. Many ball games have been won by runners breaking up double plays properly.

The idea is to disrupt the middle infielder at second base so he can't make an accurate throw to first in time to get the batter. You accomplish this by anticipating which side of the base the infielder will be on when he catches the throw, and sliding into that spot. Most of the time the shortstop will throw from the first-base side of the bag after coming across to get the throw. The second baseman will normally be on the third-base side of the bag when making his pivot. These are the areas you must slide to.

# MAKING IT SIMPLE

To make it simple, if the ball is hit to the first baseman or the second baseman, slide into the right side of the bag, and if it is hit to the third baseman or the shortstop, slide into the left side.

Because your job is to disrupt the infielder, sliding into his feet as he prepares to throw will normally get the job done. Your slide should make him throw the ball inaccurately, or at least slow down his double-play attempt. Never use a head-first slide to break up double plays. Also, never go in standing up, as there is a chance the attempted throw to first base will hit you in the face. That is not the recommended way to break up a double play. Instead try to slide into the infielder's left instep with your instep. If you hit the infielder's left leg, there probably won't be an accurate throw to first.

*Slide into the fielder and try to disrupt his throw to first base.*

# TRICK SLIDES

Most players who try trick slides are just tricking themselves. The only one that has any use is the "pop-up" slide. When using the hook slide, you have to slide past the base two to four feet before you touch it. This slide doesn't make much sense, and players today rarely use it. One slide that is interesting is the "fadeaway" slide (it also has other names). In this slide you show the infielder one hand and bring the other in to tag the bag. This slide is usually used when the ball has beaten the runner by a mile and he is going to be an easy out. It could be called the "nothing to lose" slide because there isn't much hope to bc safe anyway.

The pop-up slide is used by many players to advance quickly when there is an overthrow or other error. Use a pop-up slide:

- When the situation calls for a slide but there is some doubt if it is necessary.
- When you know you're definitely safe.
- When the probability of an overthrow or other opportunity to advance is good.

Execute the pop-up by sliding a little late (not much), and after hitting the ground push up with your legs (most players use their hands also) to regain the standing position quickly. Use the base as a stop for your lead foot. Your body should lean farther forward than in the conventional bent-leg slide.

*The hook slide requires you to go past the bag before you touch it, and is not recommended.*

*The "fadeaway" slide is used when the runner is an easy out and is hoping the fielder will miss the tag. (See also photo at right.)*

*Use the pop-up slide when you anticipate advancing to the next base because of an overthrow or misplayed ball.*

# THE HEADFIRST SLIDE, OR "PETEY"

The headfirst slide became popular in the 1960s, when Pete Rose began using it in the major leagues. In the major leagues today, many players use it almost anytime there is a close play, as in a stolen-base attempt. It has become popular with youth-league, high school, and college players all over the country. Kids quickly adopted the name "petey" after Pete Rose.

Some players who don't know how to use the bent-leg slide try to use the headfirst slide as a substitute. This is a bad idea because *you should never use a headfirst slide while sliding into home plate or while trying to break up a double play.*

All players, regardless of position or playing ability, should work on the bent-leg slide until it is easy for them. No other slides should be allowed until all players on the team can slide feetfirst safely and effectively.

When learning to slide headfirst, a player should practice on wet grass. The fundamentals involve landing on the forearms and knees first and then the chest. Players who are not accomplished at this let the chest take the full force of the fall, and this is dangerous. Injuries to the chest, neck, and back can result from this violent impact.

*In the headfirst slide, your forearms and knees absorb the shock before your chest and torso hit the ground.*

# 6
# Practice, Practice, Practice

You may think it looks easy to throw yourself headfirst at the bag like Pete Rose, or leg out that single into a double or look like Rickey Henderson breaking for second. And for some people it's easier than it is for others. But no one ever got to be good at those things without putting in the practice time. When you're talking about the fundamentals—sliding, stealing, taking a leadoff—you're talking hard work and discipline.

Unlike hitting, which you can practice on your own, you may only be able to practice your baserunning in game situations, simply because it's the unpredictable nature of baseball that makes the steals and slides so exciting. But you *can* practice in your head, by testing yourself on what you might do in various situations. This way, when you're out on the field, you'll know exactly when it's time to slide or steal that base. Of course, you'll have to practice on the field as well, but concentration will make you that much better.

Just remember, no big leaguer ever got to be great by sitting around and watching. Make a commitment, set some goals, and dedicate yourself to becoming the best ballplayer on the field!

# Index

# Index

## BASERUNNING